Honey Tree Publishing
www.honeytreepublishingus.com

For permissions, inquiries, or more information, please contact information, contact: Peter A. Whitt at whittosophy@gmail.com

Library of Congress Cataloging-in-Publication Data

Whitt, Peter. A., 1963- W.I.M.P.S. Don't Build Kingdoms

1. Religious. 2. Motivational. 3. Self-Help. 4. Trade.

Edited and Cover Designed by Dr. Tytianna Ringstaff

Printed in the United States of America

DEDICATION

I dedicate this book to two people who were amazing in my life, and throughout my life.

First, to the late Dr. Robert M. Teel. He was my high school (Melodyland Christian, Anaheim, CA) teacher, a friend and a mentor. He spoke wisdom and life to me from my Junior year of high school and throughout my adult years, especially when I became a minister. I truly want to thank him and his family for their effectual fervent prayers.

I also dedicate this book to my mom, the late Elweise Naomi (Patterson) Whitt (Union City, TN). Thank you for your keen insight into who I am supposed to be. Thank you for your prayers as well as teaching us how to pray. Forever, I will love you.

ACKNOWLEDGEMENTS

I would be remiss if I didn't thank God for placing me here, "for such a time as this." Lord, I thank you for your son and your Holy Spirit for dwelling in me all these years, "to complete a thing."

To my children, Sedrick, Ashleigh, Jenee, Jamare'on and Samar, and to my grandchildren, nephews, nieces, and cousins— Thank you to each and every one of you for your prayers. I appreciate you tremendously.

To my Carson (California) family, neighbors and friends— Always love. #Carson4Life

To my Simmons College of Kentucky (SCKY) family— Thank you for your continued support and encouragement.

To every church, every pastor and to every member that I have been blessed to fellowship with over the many years, bless you.

Finally, to my wife, Laurie Ann— Thank you for your support, your thoughts, your prayers, your encouragement and your long suffering, as well as your ability to continuously push me into excellence and not allowing me to quit, stop, or give up. I thank God that it is you that is here with me in this portion of this chapter of our life, together. "I love you most."

TABLE OF CONTENTS

FOREWORD

It is with great joy and deep respect that I write this foreword for a book that comes not just from the mind of a writer, but from the heart of a servant.

For as long as I've known Mr. Peter Whitt, I have witnessed a relentless passion for the church— not merely as a building or an institution, but as a living, breathing body of believers called to serve, love, and reach the world. This book is a reflection of that passion. It is a timely call and a thoughtful roadmap for the church to break free from its walls and step boldly into the world it was meant to transform. This work is no exception to his form and style, which has always been "words easy to be understood," combined with godly example and experience gained from many years laboring amongst those gathered unto the Lord's precious Name.

In these pages, Peter shares his personal experiences, observations, and convictions shaped by years within the church— experiences that many will recognize, and truths that challenge all of us to see beyond what is comfortable or familiar. His message is clear: the church is not just for the gathered, but for the scattered; not only for the saved, but for the seeking.

This is more than a book— it's a vision. A vision of a church that is relevant, responsive, and radically committed to expanding its reach to the masses. It is a heartfelt reminder that the Gospel was never meant to be confined, but proclaimed in every corner of our communities and nations.

Whether you are a pastor, a ministry leader, or simply someone longing for more from your church experience, I invite you to read with an open heart. Let the words within challenge you, inspire you, and most importantly, move you to action.

The church has never been more needed than it is today. And perhaps, just perhaps, this book is one of the ways God is stirring it to rise.

— Prophetess Denise Threatt

INTRODUCTION

This book, purely from my heart and led by the Holy Spirit, is not associated with or focused on any specific church or denomination. However, this book is centered on scripture and biblical references to help assess, guide, and propel church leadership from being W.I.M.P.S. to being Kingdom-builders. This book, *W.I.M.P.S.*, is an acronym noting what church leadership should strive **NOT** to be.

W – *Weak*

I – *Individual*

M – *Ministries*

P – *Perpetrating*

S – *Sanctification*

God has planted seeds within each of us, but many times we don't water the seeds because we weren't taught how to go out and till what God has been planting and watering. I remember when God first planted the seed in me to write this book. At that time, I was not fully spiritually wise. I didn't understand why God was driving me down this path and taking me on this journey.

With my spiritual growth, I now have the propensity to motivate leaders. God has called me to befriend leaders and have a listening ear because I relate to leaders without judgment or the need for recognition. Within this book, my personal experiences, interdependent with biblical teachings and scriptures, provide me with a determination to assist, help, and encourage church leadership and all people of God to grow beyond the church walls to where God has called them.

My goal is to push leaders to excellence. Leaders who are not jealous, envious, or stifling of growth freely allow their teachings to manifest while training others. It is not about following human interests but following God inside and outside of the church. When leaders send out disciples, they should return, rejoicing as the disciples did in Mark 6:12-13, when they shared their exciting experiences while out.

Furthermore, according to John 14:12 (NKJ): "Most assuredly, I say to you, He who believes in me, the works that I do, He will do also and greater works than these He will do because I go to my father." The bottom line is that we all should be aspiring to rise to new levels.

Since 1993, God has charged me to observe traditional churches and church leadership. In 2011, I preached a sermon titled "W.I.M.P.S." During this sermon, God revealed that I would write a book on that very sermon topic. It is finally here. While I do not have a degree in theology, it was not a requirement.

Over the years, my observations of many churches as a churchgoer, a choir member, a praise and worship leader, a deacon, an armor bearer, an adjutant, a minister, an elder, a servant, and a prophet, revealed that some church leaders are stagnant. During my observations, when I listened to, participated with, joined in, and communicated with church leadership, it was apparent that many church leaders were trained only in church protocol, but not in applying the biblical lessons outside church walls. Church leaders focused more on retaining people in one place, or just growing with the same people inside the four walls of the building, rather than not meeting people where they were outside the walls. Applicable training is a requirement that ministers must master to teach and train those who follow them.

Historically, Black churches have prided themselves on raising ministers and evangelists to further the church. However, ministers and evangelists aren't always prepared or encouraged to do the work they were trained to do. This is a disservice to the Kingdom-building process of God. We are all called to a ministry and required to train in that ministry to the best of our ability. Training is only effective when it's applied.

Ministry is not meant to stay in one place, such as behind the same church walls you were raised in for decades. Listening to one person, or a handful of people, for years, but not doing God's work outside of the church, contaminates the body of the church.

Many who identify as preachers, ministers, teachers, evangelists, prophets, deacons, apostles, choir members, nurses, and generally, as followers of Christ in the church, are not always following the teaching of Jesus when they limit themselves to staying in the church where they have been members all their lives. I liken it to how you would want your child to (eventually) move out of your house, to stand and face life on their own.

God purposely positions each of us, individually, so that we can meet the needs of others. Since God has called us to be great and to do great things, we need to pour out of us what God has poured into us. This is God's positioning system. God blesses us through our obedience, cheerfulness, giving, and tithing. A blessing could be a house, a car, or other material things. The fact is that the blessings we receive from God are not about us, but Kingdom work.

Some questions that may come to mind during your season of blessings are: *How do the blessings I receive from God bless others? What am I doing for God's people in the community and neighborhood? How am I sharing our testimony and speaking life into those who may be downtrodden?*

God has called each of us— no matter our ministry, denomination, religious affiliation, and financial status— to seek God's Kingdom first and bless his people (Mark 12:31). We each have an individual mandate to be the church and living examples of Jesus Christ as our Savior. However, this is not always the case across various churches, which is highly problematic.

Suppose church leaders in your church want to organize a holistic health and wellness fair, but are only requesting Christian professionals from outside of their church. This decision could be based on the church leaders' lack of encouragement of church members to venture into these professions.

Another example of the lack of preparation and support of church professionals includes the work of church musicians, singers, and psalmists. While they are celebrated for their beautiful voices, church leadership often chooses not to support the work of these artists, who could become world-renowned for their ministry and gifts. For example, many people in churches won't even purchase the music of the psalmist but want to listen to their music for free every Sunday. Church leaders should raise up and encourage people in the body of Christ to pursue their ministries and gifts professionally. They should be propelled as solo artists and musicians to become recognized globally.

On the other side, suppose you attend a church that supports the professional positions of church members as doctors, attorneys, executives, multimillionaires, teachers, musicians, and psalmists. Often, church leadership heavily relies on these individuals' monetary contributions, leaving many to abandon the church due to feeling manipulated and misled.

Reflecting on how church leaders prepare to become preachers, ministers, evangelists, and servants of Christ, I am reminded of my years in the United States Army, which I retired from after 28 years of service. Drill sergeants teach and train citizens to become soldiers. Before a soldier becomes a drill sergeant, that person undergoes rigorous training to learn how to teach, train, coach, and mentor a citizen entering basic training. Passing a test is the next step to becoming a drill sergeant, and it is not easy by far.

As a soldier, you must perform tasks to a standard and qualify to pass. This example shows how mastery leads to passing due to meeting a standard that church leadership should follow. The Bible shows us how Jesus taught, trained, and sent out His disciples to learn and apply the lessons He taught them. However, many church leaders do not follow this example. Instead, they teach biblical lessons, but do not train the next generation of church leaders to apply these lessons outside of the walls of the church building.

The training of churchgoers is often held inside the church and not outside the church. This is designed to keep people happy and excited, running and jumping up and down, not applying the training past the church walls. As a result, when faced with spiritual warfare, God's people don't know how to address the spiritual attack. Inside the walls of the church, we should train for war in preparation for a war outside the church walls.

Similar to the military, you must undergo basic training to gain confidence to face your fears, apprehensions, doubts, and confusion. With this newfound discipline, you can skillfully face any situation without hesitation.

The Roman General Vegetius said, "If you want peace, prepare for war." The military has rearranged these words when training soldiers. It now reads, "In peacetime, train for war." As you enter the military, you learn the basics. You learn how to march, how to sing cadence, how to carry your weapon, even how to clean your weapon, you learn how to exercise properly, how to receive a mission, and how to execute that mission. The military disciplines you to stand on your own two feet and have confidence. More importantly, you're trained to always travel with your "Battle Buddy."

Never leave your Battle Buddy. And, because you both have the same training, you trust your Battle Buddy the same way they trust you, because you have the same training. Allow me to pause and thank God for my Battle Buddy, Jaime Whatley of Hattiesburg, Mississippi. Yes, I still remember my Battle Buddy from 1989.

So, by the time you leave basic training, you have been trained, disciplined, and have become proficient under adverse conditions to face any situation. You entered without skills, knowledge, discipline, urgency, or timing. By the time you leave, all of that is second nature. You have a sense of urgency. You have confidence. You have the discipline for time to be on time. You can train others. You can teach others. You can encourage others to push themselves.

Church leadership should have the same mentality when teaching the basics and training leaders to stand on their own two feet. It's imperative to have a trainer who is already skilled, wise, and proficient. As a church member, you should always seek a wise teacher who teaches at your level, regardless of your background, while setting a high standard of Kingdom-building.

In Mark 6:7-13, the scriptures tell us that Jesus called the twelve to himself, sent them out two-by-two, and gave them power over unclean spirits. In other words, Jesus was their drill sergeant, trainer, and teacher. Jesus encouraged the disciples to have confidence to go out into the community and represent Him.

As leaders, we should be that example and train others on how the Lord sent out His disciples on their own, two-by-two. This means they did not stay inside the four walls of a building. They went out into the community and returned to share the Good News.

Church leaders should encourage disengagement with traditionalism, man-made doctrine, and religiosity that does not promote Kingdom-building.

We, the Kingdom of God, need church leadership not just to have a vision to further the church building or to purchase a new facility. We need church leaders to go out into the community to further the Kingdom of God. God's people are called to be with all of God's children, which requires living by example outside the church walls to go out and compel people to come to Christ (Luke 14:23).

Church leaders should reevaluate how they teach and release ministers into the community, such as through the reassessment of the training protocol of the church leadership, including teaching tithes and offerings, community charity work, and the deployment of their missionaries, outreach ministers, and evangelists. Ministering— while walking through the community— is a calling. Such ministries should be deployed throughout our communities every week. Ministers, church leadership, and church members should not just sit in the church each Sunday. They should be out in the community ministering from their divine calling. As scripture teaches us in Mark 6: 7-13, Future leaders should be trained, equipped, and deployed, just as Jesus sent out His disciples into the community.

Godly leadership sets the example for the church body. The wise and experienced in their walk must accept their responsibility as leaders, training others. This means that when the Lord sent out the disciples two-by-two, they did not stay inside the walls of a building. They went out into the community, sharing the good news with people of all walks of life. The work of Jesus and the disciples can be applied to our training and application of God's word.

If this mentality were common across all churches, our communities would have more love, peace, and contentment. This would lead to the healing, saving, and delivering of people of all walks of life through their repentance and acceptance of Jesus Christ as their Lord and Savior.

As you, dear reader, move forward in this book, I pray you will walk away with wisdom, knowledge, strength, and the confidence to encourage others. Leaders will lead, and disciples will stand on their own two feet and know they can follow the footsteps of Jesus, who trained others as Himself.

To support your growth while reading this book, the end of each chapter includes personalized reflective questions. These questions will help guide you through the scriptures and testimonies. In addition to this book, open discussions will be available in person and online to further propel the ministry's mission.

Mark 6:7-13, the scripture reads:

> And He called the twelve to Himself, and began to send them out two by two, and gave them power over unclean spirits.
>
> He commanded them to take nothing for the journey except a staff—no bag, no bread, no copper in their money belts—but to wear sandals, and not to put on two tunics.
>
> Also He said to them, "In whatever place you enter a house, stay there till you depart from that place.
>
> And whoever will not receive you nor hear you, when you depart from there, shake off the dust under your feet as a testimony against them. Assuredly, I say to you, it will be more tolerable for Sodom and Gomorrah in the day of judgment than for that city!"
>
> So they went out and preached that people should repent.
>
> And they cast out many demons, and anointed with oil many who were sick, and healed them.

CHAPTER 1

Weak

Cultish Churches vs. Kingdom-Building Churches

Growing up at the tail end of the Baby Boomer generation, we were raised in church. Back then, worship was led with a washboard, tambourine, bass drum, and even spoons—simple tools that accompanied powerful preaching. That preacher may not have had a sixth-grade education, but he knew how to rightly divide the word and serve spiritual meat that filled the soul. He was humble. Meek. Faithful. But those days are long gone.

Today, whether in a two-parent or single-parent household, there's a growing lack of commitment to taking the family to church. Maybe it's because the church has shifted. Gospel bands double as nationally recognized artists who sing sacred and secular music. Preachers chase brand deals and social media followers, swapping humility for hype and substance for style.

As a result, many in the new generation are missing out, not just on church attendance, but on the more profound benefits of knowing God for themselves and receiving instruction from a church that is truly building the Kingdom.

From Spiritual Growth to Church Business

Cultural, political, and social changes have transformed how families engage with the church. Today, the mindset in many congregations isn't focused on spiritual growth. Instead, it often centers on *church obligations*—cleaning, cooking, counting money, assembling baskets, or overseeing childcare. While necessary for operation, these distractions usually sway people from the message preached from the pulpit.

By the time many leave the church building, they've forgotten the sermon, not out of defiance, but because the church's business overshadowed the Gospel's message.

Exercising Spiritual Muscles

There's a saying: "Seven days without prayer make one weak." Without prayer, fasting, and consecration, spiritual weakness sets in.

Just as we need physical exercise to stay healthy, we also need spiritual exercise. In Acts 8, Philip left a major revival to minister to a single soul at the Lord's direction. That was obedience, guided by spiritual conditioning. He didn't rely on physical fitness but on spiritual strength to hear and respond to the Holy Spirit's call.

Paul, too, modeled the life of a spiritually disciplined disciple. We are called to live the same way.

The Cost of Spiritual Weakness

Spiritual weakness makes room for sin. Romans 6:1–2 reminds us not to continue in sin so that grace may abound. That mindset—of abusing grace—is far from God's plan. As we move away from sin, our faith strengthens. Our hope becomes action. Our confidence in the Spirit becomes our guide.

Still, many confuse hope with faith. Hope says, "I wish things would get better." Faith says, "I'll move forward even if I can't see how." Hebrews 11:1 defines faith as "the substance of things hoped for, the evidence of things not seen." Joseph modeled that faith when he said, "What you meant for evil, God meant for good" (Genesis 50:20). Martin Luther called faith "a daring confidence in God's grace, so sure and certain that the believer would stake his life on it a thousand times."

Faith isn't just something we have—it's something we must exercise. According to Romans 12:3, God gives each of us a *measure* of faith. But without spiritual training, we may never use it.

Churches Built on Emotion, Not Equipping

Many churches aren't teaching people how to operate in faith. Instead, they center on emotional experiences—shouting, running, hollering—rather than training and discipling believers to *do the work*. Jesus didn't just preach; He prepared and sent out the seventy-two, who returned excited about the lives they had touched.

The church is meant to be a training ground, where people are spiritually equipped to go into the world, healing, teaching, and building the Kingdom. Unfortunately, today's church leadership is often more concerned with building platforms than building people.

What Is Kingdom-Building?

It's time for leaders to seriously ask: *What is our mission? What is Kingdom-building?* A Kingdom-building church prepares people to serve others and spread the Gospel, not just preserve church traditions. In contrast, a cultish church promotes man-made doctrine, public shame, and judgment under the guise of "holiness."

In cultish churches, you might see:

- Public shaming during sacred moments like prayer
- No intercessory training or true prayer warriors
- Judgment of sin without spiritual restoration
- Leadership that enforces control instead of nurturing growth

James 5:16 teaches us that "the effective, fervent prayer of a righteous man avails much." Prayer warriors are not called to condemn but to cover.

Galatians 6:1-2 echoes this: we are to restore one another with gentleness. The church should be a place of protection, not punishment.

Confronting Traditionalism and Gender Bias

Traditionalists often believe that there is only one way to God—one that requires rigid rules, steps, and church-based classes. They won't enter marginalized neighborhoods. Meanwhile, a new generation understands the power of "speaking life" and meets people where they are.

But many churches are still rooted in gendered traditions that limit women and uphold double standards. Some teach that women must remain silent in church (1 Corinthians 14:34–35), or wear long skirts while men go unchecked in modesty. This kind of cultish doctrine distorts scripture to control rather than to elevate.

Yet, Joel 2:28 tells us clearly: "I will pour out My Spirit on all flesh; your sons and daughters shall prophesy." God does not withhold His Spirit based on gender, age, or culture. Galatians 3:28 reinforces this: in Christ, we are all one.

Moving from Cliques to Community

Many cultish churches focus on:

- Membership numbers
- Gossip and cliques
- Social status and appearance
- Financial contributions
- Church drama over community engagement

This isn't Kingdom work. It's self-preservation.

A friend once told me: "Our job is to catch the fish. We should let God clean the fish." That's the job of the disciple—to love and gather. As Jesus taught, "Love your neighbor as yourself" (Mark 12:31).

If churches want to grow healthily and sustainably, leaders must be willing to train themselves out of a position and equip the next generation.

A Generation Ready to Lead

The global events of 2020—police brutality, protests, a pandemic, and political unrest—shook the foundation of many churches. As buildings closed, people found God for themselves. They opened their Bibles, discovered their spiritual identity, and began understanding Kingdom work.

The church's role now is to equip and train these individuals to prepare them for the work of the ministry. The next generation has passion, influence, and social awareness. They are ready. They just need guidance and release.

God elevates whom He chooses. And if He is in everything, even the chaos, we must see Him in everything, and respond accordingly.

Reflective Questions

1. Is your church building the Kingdom or simply maintaining traditions?

2. How does your church train people to live out their faith?

3. Are you exercising your own spiritual muscles?

4. Are you willing to release others to lead, or are you holding onto power?

5. Are you truly operating in faith, or just hoping things will change?

CHAPTER 2

Individual

Having Faith and Walking in the Spirit

What does it really mean to *have faith* and *walk in the Spirit*?

Walking in the Spirit is more than a spiritual phrase—it is the posture and power of a believer's daily life. It is our divine compass, our covering, and our armor. It's how we navigate life's trials and triumphs with the assurance that God guides our every step.

Faith is the foundation of that walk. But faith, by design, is personal. It's an individual journey—just like the moment Jesus said, *"Here I am, send me"* (Isaiah 6:8). Every believer has their own cross to bear, their own calling, and their own path. Just as Isaiah, John, Peter, and Paul were called up to commune with God, so too are we. "God is Spirit, and those who worship Him must worship in spirit and truth" (John 4:24).

Faith Starts in the Secret Place

Developing a spiritual walk with God begins with time alone in His presence. It's cultivated in prayer, fasting, consecration, and quiet communion. It's when no one is looking that we hear the clearest. That's where purpose is revealed.

Unfortunately, some traditional church models hinder individual spiritual development by focusing more on what the church needs than the person's needs. But God doesn't dwell in buildings made by hands (Acts 7:48–49; Acts 17:24). His Spirit moves freely and personally.

A personal relationship with God saves us, not a mundane and meaningless routine. Your calling may not look like someone else's, and that's by design. When we understand our purpose, we begin to understand our role within the larger body of Christ.

Walking in Purpose, Not Position

Walking in the Spirit allows us to move with divine purpose—whether that means becoming a chef, a teacher, a doctor, or an attorney. Your profession doesn't exempt you from ministry—it's where your ministry begins.

Sadly, many churches have failed to equip believers for this spiritual impact. Instead of raising up leaders to transform cities, systems, and communities, some churches simply expect members to give more while offering little in return. This imbalance is why so many congregants feel disillusioned and disconnected.

You don't have to be a pastor to make a difference. You just have to be willing. Churches should cultivate attorneys, educators, grant writers, political advocates—people with the spiritual wisdom and practical tools to support God's work.

The Decline of Community Impact

When we stop going out into the community, we stop building the Kingdom. Many churches today expect people to enter the building, forgetting that Jesus said to *go out* and compel them.

We've lost connection with our neighbors. We haven't trained this generation to build relationships with those around them. Instead, the same faithful few are asked to give, serve, and sacrifice, often with little spiritual nourishment in return. Eventually, they burn out, grow bitter, or walk away.

Ministry Is Sacrifice

Jesus warned in Mark 6:10–11 that not everyone will receive us. Still, we are called to go, speak, and serve. Ministry is effort. Ministry is rejection. But it's also compassion, empathy, and perseverance.

James 2:20 reminds us *that* faith without works is dead. Faith isn't just belief—it's action. It's stepping out before we see the outcome and trusting God to provide. It's laying hands, casting out demons, and speaking life, whether in a sanctuary, a hospital room, a courtroom, or a classroom.

Everyone Has a Role in Kingdom-Building

Romans 12:3 says God gives each of us a measure of faith. That means we all have something to contribute—regardless of title, tenure, or tradition.

Mark 16:17 assures us that "signs will follow those who believe." Not just apostles, bishops, or elders—but believers. True Kingdom-building doesn't happen through hierarchy. It happens through belief.

Ephesians 4:7–16 shows us that Christ gave us apostles, prophets, evangelists, pastors, and teachers to equip the saints for works of service. Our job as leaders is to recognize, affirm, and activate the gifts inside every believer. When each part of the body does its work, the entire Church grows in love and maturity.

Abraham and Isaac: A Model of Faith and Trust

Consider Abraham and Isaac in Genesis 22. Abraham was told to sacrifice his son, a command that seems unimaginable. But both father and son modeled radical faith.

Isaac, likely a young man around 12 or 13, trusted his father deeply. He carried the wood. He asked about the lamb. He allowed himself to be bound. And even when Abraham raised the knife, Isaac stayed. That's not just obedience—it's trust. It's faith.

So, who had more faith? Abraham, who believed God would provide? Or Isaac, who trusted the man who trusted God?

The lesson here is simple: We each hear from God differently, but we're all called to trust Him deeply.

A Serious Walk for a Serious Call

Dr. Charles Stanley once said, "A Christian life is serious business. You have to be serious about God. You have to be serious about Christ. And you have to be serious about purpose."

But many people play church. We dress right. We say the right things. We wear a Christian mask. All the while, the enemy is watching and waiting.

Like Job, the more we walk with God, the more the enemy tries to shake us. Church leadership especially must guard their spirit through prayer, not just as a formality but as a lifeline. And yet many stand at the altar pretending they're fine when they're spiritually depleted.

The Power of Prayer—Personal and Corporate

James 5:16 says, "The effective, fervent prayer of a righteous man avails much." That kind of prayer isn't reserved for the pastor. It's for every believer.

Corporate prayer is when believers come together, regardless of title or position, to intercede for one another. The Church functions as a body, covering every part in love. There is no hierarchy in these moments—just honesty, healing, and humility.

Imagine a church where:

- Members pray openly for their leaders.
- Leaders confess their needs without fear of gossip.
- Prayer is the first response, not the last resort.

That's a spiritually equipped church. That's Kingdom culture. It's time to move beyond routines and apply God's Word.

Reflective Questions

1. How can you apply lessons from church or scripture to your current season in life?

2. Reflect on a sermon that recently resonated with you. How does that message apply today?

CHAPTER 3
Ministries

Chosen and Called for Purpose

We are the chosen ones. God chose us before the foundation of the world to be holy, blameless, and adopted into sonship through Jesus Christ. Ephesians 1:4-5 says, "Just as He chose us in Him before the foundation of the world..." This scripture affirms that our calling is intentional, divine, and purposeful. Everything we do should reflect God's glory. Our witness is not limited to the church but should extend into every interaction.

Living as a Reflection of God

It's one thing to talk the talk, but can you walk the walk? We can look good on the outside, dress up, and attend events, but how we carry ourselves in conversation and conduct determines whether people see Christ in us. Similarly, quoting scripture without context or compassion can repel rather than attract others to God. We must meet people where they are. We are living epistles—our lives are the scriptures some people will read.

As 2 Corinthians 3:3 tells us, "You are an epistle of Christ." Our witness must be honest: "I fall short, but God forgives and restores." Psalm 103:12 reminds us, "As far as the east is from the west, so far has He removed our transgressions from us." And when we sin, 1 John 2:1 assures us that we have an advocate in Jesus Christ.

Discovering God's Purpose for Your Life

Every person has a divine calling. As leaders, we mentor and train others to discover and pursue their God-ordained purpose. Jeremiah 1:5 says, "Before I formed you in the womb I knew you," Jeremiah 29:11 confirms that His plans for us are filled with hope.

Understanding purpose begins with seeking God. Matthew 6:33 teaches us to "seek first the Kingdom." Purpose isn't only found in church titles but in how we live, work, and serve. Ministries can start anywhere: at home, on the job, in the streets. Disciples are known by their love, not their position.

Recognizing God's Process

Purpose is often revealed through testing. Job's story reminds us that while Satan may be allowed to test us, he cannot destroy us without God's permission (Job 1:8, 1:12). Trials are often the tools God uses to shape our faith.

Lessons Learned in the Military: A Place of Training

The military has a model called "Train the Trainer." A leader teaches someone who can then teach others. Ministry should function the same way. Paul said in Philippians 4:11, "I have learned to be content in all circumstances." We are called to be content, faithful, and fruitful—inside and outside the church. A minister should, essentially, teach or train prospective leaders to seek God for themselves and understand why they face difficult situations, regardless of their abundance or lack. As the Apostle Paul stated in Philippians 4:11 - _**Not that I speak regarding need, for I have learned to be content in whatever state I am in**_.

Ministry exists beyond the church's four walls, not just inside. We see this in scripture when Jesus travels the land, ministering to God's people outside the temple. This is a key example of how Outside the church is where ministry is refined through humble actions and deeds, serving God's people.

Luke 19:5: And when Jesus came to the place, He looked up and saw him, and said to him, "Zacchaeus, make haste and come down, for today I must stay at your house."

Jesus was not in a temple, church, or sanctuary. He was in the village, streets, neighborhood, and the community. He was where the people lived. That is ministry. To reach people, you must meet them where they are. This example shows how Jesus sees people without judgment and how he meets their needs. We are to do the same by modeling Jesus' example as the ultimate minister, as the Son of God.

Leadership Training

It all goes back to training. Preaching is preaching, and we want to encourage the congregation to stand a little stronger. But training teaches you how to apply the message you receive from the sermon daily. That's training.

So, how do we go about training an individual? The training is repetition. The repetition, when we're faced with it, we should know it by heart. We should teach our children how to give our Easter speech. How do you teach them to remember their easter speech? They had to repeat it. They had to be talked to. You had to teach them what they were going to say. You had to read it with them. You had to have them say it on their own. That was training. Repetition. Then, on the performance day, they would either be too nervous and shy away, forget a line or part, or be successful and say the speech. Either way, it happens; they at least attempted, and that is what God applauds. He applauds the individual for at least attempting.

"You and I are responsible for the truth that we hear," said Rev. Dr. Ruth Wilson, Pastor of Shekinah Glory Ministries, Louisville, Kentucky. When we hear the truth and our spirit agrees with it, knowing it is from God, we are responsible for taking that message forward. We must do the work required with an unwavering faith in God.

Jesus' Ministry Was in the Streets

Luke 19:5 tells us how Jesus called Zacchaeus down from a tree and visited his home. Ministry happens outside the sanctuary. We must model Jesus, meeting people where they are with love, grace, and truth.

Training Requires Repetition

Training is not a one-time event. It is repetitive, deliberate, and rooted in relationship. Spiritual training involves practice, patience, and performance, like children learning an Easter speech. Even if you stumble, God sees and honors your attempt.

Ministry in Action: Four Foundational Truths

1. **Ministry Is Effort** (Acts 8:26-40): True ministry involves going beyond the church walls. Like Philip, who left a revival to minister to one Ethiopian man, we must be ready to act when God speaks, even in unexpected places.

2. **Ministry Is sacrifice** (2 Timothy 4:1-5): Preach in and out of season. The calling comes with discomfort. Long-suffering builds strength. We must also intercede for others, just as Jesus sent disciples in pairs for mutual support.

3. **Ministry Is Rejection** (Isaiah 53:5-8): Jesus was rejected so we could be accepted. As we follow Him, we too will face rejection. But rejection is often redirection—a tool God uses to elevate us spiritually.

4. **Ministry Is Compassion and Empathy** (Mark 6:7-13): Jesus sent out disciples without titles or positions. They preached, healed, and delivered by faith. Leaders must train others to go and do the same.

The Weight of Misaligned Ministry

When churches misalign with Kingdom purpose, they face different kinds of bankruptcy:

- **Spiritual Bankruptcy** – Losing spiritual fervor due to weak prayer lives (Matthew 26:40).

- **Financial Bankruptcy** – Mismanaging church funds or relying solely on government aid.

- **Membership Bankruptcy** – People leaving silently due to lack of trust or disconnection.

- **Talent Bankruptcy** – Leaders burning out or failing to grow spiritually.

Reclaiming True Ministry

God does not need mega-churches. He needs mega-faith. Revelation shows that the smallest churches did the most impactful work. Phillip's example in Acts 8:26-40 and Romans 10:14-15 reminds us that people cannot believe in a God they've never heard of and won't hear without a messenger.

Let us be messengers, ministers, and mentors who teach others how to walk boldly in purpose. As God trains us, we must train others. When we pass the baton, we empower the next generation to do even greater things for the Kingdom.

Reflective Questions

1. Who has God called you to be, and what has He called you to do?

2. What barriers have prevented you from fully walking in your purpose?

3. How can you better train or equip others for Kingdom work?

4. Are you actively listening for God's direction in your daily life?

5. What type of "bankruptcy"—spiritual, financial, membership, or talent—has your ministry experienced, and how can it be restored?

CHAPTER 4
Perpetrating

A Shift in Worship: The Pandemic and Digital Giving

During the global pandemic of 2020, physically attending church became impossible. The shutdown forced churches to enter the digital world. Many congregations had to adapt quickly, learning to accept electronic funds in a culture where giving a tangible dollar bill on a plate was still the norm. For some, it wasn't considered real if it wasn't placed on an offering plate. However, the format of giving is not nearly as important as the motivation and the biblical foundation behind it. Churches and congregants alike had to reexamine their understanding of tithes and offerings.

Understanding the Purpose of Tithing

Tithing is not merely about money but a spiritual act of obedience and gratitude. When someone blesses you—through prayer, service, or support—your desire to bless others often stems from a heart of thankfulness. Giving can be directed toward individuals, ministries, charities, or those who intercede on your behalf. Scripture provides the foundation for tithing, most notably in Genesis 14:18–20, where Abram gave Melchizedek, the priest of God Most High, a tithe. This was a freewill offering of honor and obedience, inspired not by obligation but divine reverence.

Becoming a Cheerful Giver

In 2 Corinthians 9:6–10, we are reminded of the principle of sowing and reaping. "God loves a cheerful giver," the scripture reads. When we give cheerfully and freely, we open ourselves to receive God's abundance—not just in finances but in righteousness, purpose, and provision. The Apostle Paul writes that God supplies seed to the sower and bread for food and promises to increase our store of seed and enlarge the harvest of our righteousness.

Misuse and Misunderstanding in the Modern Church

Yet despite the clear biblical teaching, not all churches follow it. Too often, leaders are entrenched in man-made doctrines that misuse the concept of tithing, pressuring congregants to give sacrificially, even when it places them under financial strain. Regardless of their circumstances, some are asked to stand and give $50 or $100. This kind of coercion misrepresents the purpose of giving.

Giving Within Your Means

True tithing should reflect an individual's financial capacity. For example, if someone earns $50,000 a year, their ten percent tithe would be $5,000 annually, roughly $420 monthly or $105 weekly. Everything beyond that is considered an offering. However, it's not just about money. Time and talent are equally significant forms of giving. God honors both. Serving in ministry, sowing into the community, or mentoring others are also sacred acts of giving.

The Joseph Model: Saving and Stewardship

We must also consider the biblical principle of stewardship. In Genesis 41:34–36, Joseph instructed Pharaoh to save one-fifth of the grain during years of plenty to prepare for a future famine. This strategy preserved not only Egypt but also the surrounding nations. Churches today must adopt similar wisdom. Rather than constantly asking congregants for more, churches should save and store a portion of their tithes for future needs.

Giving from the Heart: Offerings and Their Purpose

Offerings are distinct from tithes. They are not commanded but given freely and joyfully. Unfortunately, many churches continuously plead for more offerings, causing guilt among those already financially stretched. Individuals on fixed incomes—such as seniors, disabled persons, or those living paycheck to paycheck—should not feel ashamed for giving what they can. The Apostle Paul wrote in 2 Corinthians 9:6–7 that we should give as we purpose in our hearts, not grudgingly or under compulsion, for God loves a cheerful giver.

Practicing Consistent and Sincere Giving

However, giving must be consistent and sincere. If you tithe faithfully and give offerings as purposed in your heart, there is no reason to feel guilt for not giving more. What matters is that your giving is rooted in obedience and joy, not performance or pressure.

When Leaders Lead by Example

Church leadership must lead by example. Many do not tithe themselves, resulting in spiritual and financial imbalance in the congregation. When leaders do not model stewardship, there is "no meat in the storehouse." In his leadership, Joseph saved one-fifth of Egypt's harvest for seven years, preparing for a future drought. This practice sustained not only his people but entire nations.

Giving with a Purpose and a Plan

Churches should likewise set aside some of their tithes and offerings with a specific mission in mind. Whether supporting domestic violence survivors, building community housing, or feeding the hungry, churches must steward God's resources with vision and discipline. In Matthew 6:1–8, Jesus reminds us that true giving is not about being seen by others—it's about pleasing God, who sees in secret and rewards openly.

The Church as a Spiritual and Physical Storehouse

God's Word in Genesis 41:56–57 shows that Joseph opened the storehouses to feed the people when famine came. In the same way, churches today should be prepared to meet the needs of their communities. Tithes and offerings are not to accumulate wealth for show, but to serve people who are hungry, homeless, hurting, or in crisis.

Empowering Communities through Economic Justice

Economic empowerment must also be part of the church's mission. Bishop Vaughn McLaughlin once taught that believers empowered to run businesses properly will bless the church. When God increases us, we should return a portion of that increase to His house. Leadership, therefore, must not be jealous or threatened by those who rise. Instead, leaders should encourage and pray for those whom God is elevating. Romans 2:11 says, "For there is no partiality with God." God can use anyone.

Faithful Through Trials: Joseph's Legacy

Joseph understood this. Despite betrayal, enslavement, false accusations, and imprisonment, he remained faithful. He later declared in Genesis 50:20, "You meant evil against me; but God meant it for good... to save many people alive."

This is the true purpose of the Church: to endure hardship so others may be saved. Joseph's life demonstrates that faithful stewardship and obedience can change nations.

Reviving the Church's Original Call

The Azusa Street Revival and the Civil Rights Movement are historical reminders that the Black church once led with compassion, justice, and unity. Today's church must return to that model—raising new leaders, confronting violence, and addressing poverty, domestic abuse, and community trauma. Sadly, many churches now require application forms to prove someone is poor before offering any food, clothing, shelter, or financial assistance. This is not the Church that Christ modeled.

Breaking Cycles of Guilt and Misuse

Too often, congregants are manipulated into giving through fear or guilt. But Malachi 3:10 tells us to "bring all the tithes into the storehouse, that there may be food in My house." Literal and spiritual food feeds those in need. Joseph's approach of storing 1/5 allowed Egypt to bless other nations. Churches today must adopt that mindset.

Renewal Through Reflection and Reform

The pandemic did not close the Church; God allowed it to be exposed. During that time, churches continued collecting tithes. But after reopening, many returned to the same broken systems. It is time to reform. Doing the same thing over and over while expecting a different result is, as many say, the definition of insanity.

A Humble Return to God's Instruction

The Church must go beyond being seen as a good choir, building, or social spot. We must reengage with the community. If not, we risk being seen as disconnected, irrelevant, or even self-righteous. If people do not see your church outside the four walls, they won't be compelled to enter.

Some church leaders, including Pastors Dr. Fred Price and Dr. Creflo Dollar, have acknowledged past misguided teachings on tithing, and they have repented. That humility and correction are what the Church needs. God will honor us when we tithe and give properly, with purpose, love, and stewardship.

Reflective Questions

1. Are you tithing and offering with understanding, or out of guilt or obligation?

2. Is your church stewarding its tithes and offerings wisely?

3. In what ways can your church save, store, and distribute funds to bless others?

4. How does your giving align with God's purpose for your life?

5. What legacy of giving and service are you leaving behind?

CHAPTER 5
Sanctification

Training and Releasing for Kingdom Expansion

As a spiritual leader, the goal is to train, teach, and celebrate when it's their time to leave this part of the vineyard. The Kingdom of God expands by releasing others into a dying world to expand His work wherever God leads them. Too often, leaders assume that people who have been in the church for a long time should remain there forever. But God does not call us to hoard people; He calls us to send them. Whether they are starting another church or doing outreach in another city, we must celebrate their release.

Proverbs 3:5–6 states, "Trust in the LORD with all your heart, And lean not on your own understanding; In all your ways acknowledge Him, And He shall direct your paths." When God moves someone, we leaders should not view it as a loss but as Kingdom expansion. Jealousy and envy have no room in ministry. Instead, we should celebrate our role in preparing them for what lies ahead.

The Heart of a Leader: Celebration, Not Competition

Any person can feel jealousy and envy, and church leaders are no exception. We often feel a sense of hurt when someone leaves, even when there is no malice. But when someone is called to another part of the Kingdom, we must support and bless their journey. As the saying goes, "A preacher has got to preach" (Anthony Hampton).

Whether a person is called to lead, evangelize, teach, or simply rest and renew before being released for a purpose, their presence and departure should be met with encouragement. As 2 Corinthians 3:3 says, "You are an Epistle of Christ." People read us—our witness, humility, love, and ability to reconcile and restore.

Walking in Purpose: Overcoming the Flesh

So, the questions become: *How do we overcome our flesh? How do we get to our "nevertheless" moment?*

Philippians 4:6 reminds us:

> "Be anxious for nothing, but in everything by prayer and supplication, with thanksgiving, let your requests be made known to God." Jesus Himself prayed this kind of prayer. In Luke 22:42, He said, "Father, if it is Your will, take this cup away from Me. Nevertheless, not My will, but Yours, be done."

This was Jesus' moment of overcoming the flesh. He showed us that prayer is the pathway to overcoming. Overcoming the flesh is likely the most challenging battle we face, and Jesus, God in flesh, modeled that even He struggled. But He obeyed.

1 Samuel 15:22 says, "Behold, to obey is better than sacrifice." Overcoming the flesh means obeying God's will, even when painful, unfamiliar, or uncomfortable.

Illumination Through the Word

Psalm 119:105 declares, "Your word is a lamp to my feet And a light to my path." Staying on the path requires discipline. Like Dorothy in *The Wizard of Oz*, we must remain on the illuminated road, avoiding the detours and distractions that try to pull us off course. And when we get off track, the word hidden in our hearts brings us back.

Psalm 119:11 says, "Your word I have hidden in my heart, That I might not sin against You." Scripture is our anchor. When discouraged, God's Word reminds us of who we are and where we're going.

Ordered Steps and Leadership Training

Psalm 119:133 says, "Direct my steps by Your word, And let no iniquity have dominion over me." This is more than a verse—it's a daily prayer for leaders. Like in the military, spiritual leadership requires training, discipline, and preparation to lead and release others.

In the military, rank is earned through education, experience, knowledge, and discipline. The church should mirror this preparation:

- **Education** – Learning the Word and church doctrine.
- **Experience** – Applying the Word and leading in real-life situations.
- **Knowledge** – Rightly dividing the Word of Truth.
- **Discipline** – Staying composed and committed, even under pressure.

A leader who has proven themselves in these areas should be recognized and released when it is time, just as a Ministry Mentor Elder Stephens trained me to administer communion before I left Germany. He gave me the wisdom, knowledge, and experience to stand on my own.

Letting Go of Familiarity

It is not for all of us to be born in the same church and die in the same church. That is not growth—that is comfort and familiarity. Growth comes from being equipped and then released to go forward.

John 11:9–10 reminds us, "Are there not twelve hours in the day? If anyone walks in the day, he does not stumble... But if one walks at night, he stumbles, because the light is not in him." When the light of Christ is in us, we can walk confidently wherever He sends us.

The Harm of Shame in the Church

Sadly, many churches still practice public shaming. One example comes from a church in Virginia where a young woman was forced to stand before the congregation and apologize for becoming pregnant before marriage. Worse still, the pastor announced she would not be celebrated with a baby shower or supported by the church.

Where was the man who fathered the child? Why was he not held accountable in the same way?

This mentality inspired this book: W.I.M.P.S. – Weak Individual Ministries Perpetrating Sanctification. Churches should be spaces of love, covering, and restoration, not public humiliation.

John 8:3–11 speaks to this very issue. The Pharisees brought a woman caught in adultery before Jesus. They were ready to stone her, but Jesus challenged them, "He who is without sin among you, let him throw a stone at her first." One by one, they left.

When Jesus asked the woman where her accusers were, she replied, "No one, Lord." Jesus responded, "Neither do I condemn you; go and sin no more."

This is the heart of Christ. This is what leaders must model. We are not called to condemn but to restore.

Final Thoughts

Leadership is not about control—it's about trust. It's about equipping others and releasing them in faith. It's about recognizing when God is shifting someone, celebrating that shift, and knowing the Kingdom is expanding.

We must teach, train, and release—not hoard and hinder. In doing so, we become true examples of Christ, reflecting His love, discipline, and grace.

Reflective Questions

1. Have I ever struggled with releasing someone from my ministry or leadership circle? What emotions surfaced, and how did I respond?

2. What does it mean for me to have a "nevertheless" moment? When have I chosen obedience over comfort?

3. In what ways am I training others for Kingdom expansion rather than keeping them close out of fear or familiarity?

4. Are there any areas where I've allowed shame or judgment to overshadow grace in my leadership?

5. What steps can I take to ensure I illuminate Christ's love in both word and deed, even in professional settings?

CONCLUSION

The Purpose Behind This Book

While writing this book, I have learned a lot about myself, further developing wisdom, leading me away from bitterness, anger, and hostility toward the church that could develop from such observations. Thus, this book was never intended to attack the church. Instead, it is a clarion call to revive church leadership's purpose, passion, and posture in alignment with God's Kingdom.

Like any profession, longevity comes from loyalty. However, loyalty to a building or a person should never outweigh loyalty to the calling and mission of Christ. Our devotion must extend beyond four walls. Fellowship with like-minded believers is essential, but engaging those who don't believe is the true work of evangelism.

Throughout the chapters, we examined how training, discipline, spiritual maturity, and purpose must undergird the structure of church leadership. From the dangers of stagnation to the power of personal spiritual growth, this book is meant to realign the church's mission with the example of Jesus Christ.

A Diverse and Active Church

The High Definition (HD) Church is diverse in age, generation, nationalities, and race because that's how heaven is. It's not all African American people on one side and all Caucasian people on the other side. The church should reflect a heavenly vision of unity and diversity. Kingdom work doesn't have a demographic filter.

Dr. Henry Claire said it best: "Everybody, do everything." That's how he raised us and how he pastored us. His church may be small in number, but it's still standing. Everyone is working, everyone is serving. We can accomplish great things when we adopt the mindset that many hands make light work.

Celebrating and Sending

True leaders celebrate when others are called to move forward in their journey. We train to release, not retain. The church is not a place to collect people but to equip and send them out.

As discussed, leadership must equip others through education, experience, knowledge, and discipline. Like the military, leaders are promoted and moved to new assignments. Spiritual leaders must follow this model, identifying and training those called to lead and releasing them when God says it is time.

Confronting Church Hurt and Misalignment

Yes, there are failures in the church. There are moments when leaders shame instead of support. There are churches more focused on entertainment, titles, or control than on empowering people. But just as Jesus refused to condemn the woman caught in adultery, we must learn to minister from a place of grace, not guilt.

Many have been wounded by churches perpetuating tradition over transformation, control over calling, and systems over the Spirit. But that does not mean we abandon the church. It means we correct its course.

A Church on Mission

In conclusion, the church's mission is to preach to teach, teach to reach, and then send out. Preaching should prepare believers to live transformed lives, to reach into their families and communities with God's love, and to be sent into the world as Kingdom ambassadors.

Our preaching should equip the congregation to reach beyond the church walls and teach the purpose of God's children for Kingdom-building.

That is the essence of ministry. That is the heart of God.

Reflective Questions

1. How can my church better reflect the diversity of God's Kingdom?

2. Am I willing to release people when God calls them to something new?

3. What systems or traditions may hinder the Spirit's movement in my ministry?

4. Who am I equipping to be sent out?

5. What does a successful church look like through the lens of Kingdom impact, not just attendance?